The Bumper b3ta Book of Sick Jokes

The Bumper b3ta Book of Sick Jokes

Compiled by Rob Manuel

FRIDAY BOOKS

First published in Great Britain in 2006 by Friday Books
An imprint of The Friday Project Limited
83 Victoria Street, London SW1H0HW

www.thefridayproject.co.uk
www.fridaybooks.co.uk

ISBN 10 – 1-905548-28-1
ISBN 13 – 978-1-905548-28-6

British Library Cataloguing in Publication Data

A catalogue record for this book is available from the British Library

Designed and produced by Jason Taylor
www.liquorice-creative.co.uk

The Publisher's policy is to use paper manufactured from sustainable sources

Contents

Introduction

Oh dear God, how are we supposed to introduce this? In your hands you are holding the most depraved, foul and offensive collection of jokes collected in one book.

You're probably expecting us to write something to justify this collection aren't you? Something erudite and wordy that explains that these jokes are a reflection of society's pressure points and fears? Nope. Sorry. You'll have to look elsewhere for that stuff, for we know the sordid truth: Sick jokes are guilty pleasures shared when you think no one who may be offended is listening.

And we've got the whole damn lot of them.

Even the ones where they said, 'No, you can't print that, they'll fire-bomb the publishers'.

But don't worry. If you do find yourself getting nauseated, just turn to the 'panic page' on p 168 where we've stuck some nice fluffy jokes and a picture of a kitten. See? All better now.

Enjoy the book!

How this book was made

Every joke in this book was submitted by the public. That's the cunning get out clause. This is your book! Not ours!

You see, we have a quite famous website called b3ta.com, and we asked our visitors to send in their sickest jokes. And they did, in bloody droves. Two and a half thousand of them to be exact, and when we threw away the crap ones we're left with this lot here.

Then we did the clever bit; we asked the site readers to send in illustrations to make the book look pretty. There's a full list of credits at the back, so if you want to give these people work, you should be able to find them.

So that was our dream. Make a book simply by asking the Internet to do it for us. And it worked. Lazy sods? Us? Yep.

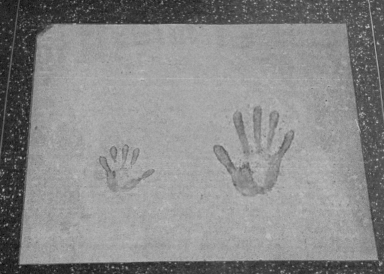

Celebrity and news events

Whenever there is a news event involving a major disaster or a celebrity there is always a joke being told in the pub, texted on a phone or sent by email. Here are some of your favourites.

Did you know that Jeremy Beadle has a tiny cock?
On the other hand, it's massive.

**What was the last thing to go through
Kurt Cobain's mind as he pulled the trigger?**

A bullet.

**Roy Castle finally made it
into the Guinness Book of Records.**

They gave him 6 months to live
and he did it in 2.

Elton John is getting a divorce.

He found out his husband was having sex
behind his back.

**What did Robert Maxwell
and Freddie Mercury have in common?**

They were both bumped off by dodgy seamen.

**What's pink and fluffy and hasn't
moved in years?**

Freddie Mercury's slippers.

What's black and shoots across a room?

Marvin Gaye's dad.

"Hi, I'm Simon Weston and I'd like to talk to you about my new grill...

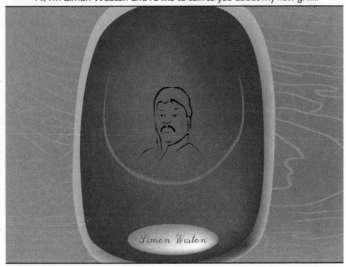

...it's so good I put my face on it!"

What's pink and smells of piss?

Barbara Cartland.

What's the difference between Jill Dando and a white shirt?

The white shirt survived the doorstep challenge.

Jill Dando's husband wanted to paint the front door red.

She was dead against it though.

What's black, white and starving?

Jill Dando's cat.

They are going to make a film about Harold Shipman starring Robert De Niro.

It's called *The Old Dear Hunter.*

Guard: 'What would you like to drink?'
Harold Shipman: 'A nice whiskey would be great.'
Guard: 'What would you about you?'
Myra Hindley: 'I'd love some red wine.'
Guard: 'What would you like?'
Fred West: 'I could murder some Tennants.'

Ian Brady says to the prison guard, 'I'm pissed off, I haven't had a holiday in years!'.

To which the guard says, 'Come off it Brady, a few years ago we took you up to Saddleworth Moor, you had 3 days up there – all those wide open spaces and fresh clean air'.

Brady replies, 'Fair enough, but what kind of holiday was that with the kids under me feet?'.

What sits in the corner of the lounge and crackles?
Rod Hull's television.

What's Rod Hull's favourite washing powder?
Aerial.

What were Rod Hull's last words?
'Grab hold of that fucking gutter, Emu!'

What's black and slid down Nelson's Column?
Winnie Mandela.

What's green and 50 feet tall?
Nelson Mandela's lawn.

Dancing on your ceiling

▶ Ghosts are often claimed to be hallucinations. Certainly people can be tricked into 'seeing' things that do not exist. Stare at the cross in the centre of Lionel Ritchie's face, while you count slowly to 120. Then look at a plain ceiling. You should 'see' a phantom Lionel Ritchie dancing on the ceiling. If the image has not faded within 5 minutes, consult an optomexorcist.

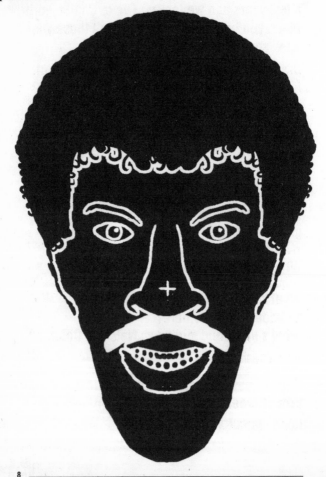

What's grey and smells of curry?

John Major's dick.

What do you call a bird that can't fly?

That bird off Holby City.

What's the Queen Mum and a cock got in common?

They both go hard after three strokes.

What's blue, hangs from the ceiling and doesn't fit anymore?

Ian Curtis.

Gene Pitney's undertakers have said that it will take 10 weeks to make him a coffin from oak… or 24 hours from balsa…

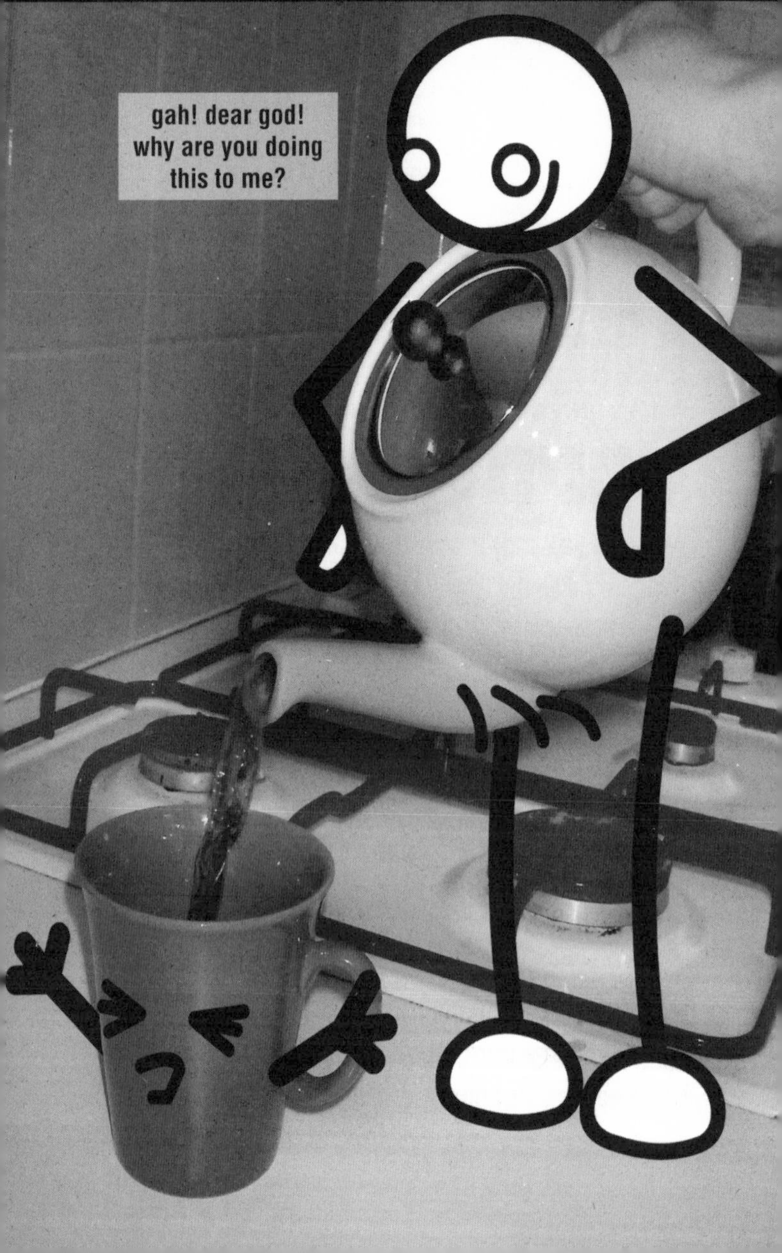
gah! dear god!
why are you doing
this to me?

Michael Barrymore

Poor old Barrymore, crucified by the tabloids for a crime he didn't commit. That didn't stop the public voting him second in the 2005 Celebrity Big Brother. We haven't heard from him since but we suspect he'll be back. Anyway, there is always panto…

Have you heard that Michael Barrymore has got a new TV show?

Only Pools and Corpses.

Two dead terrorists were found in Michael Barrymore's swimming pool.

They were suicide bummers.

The Beatles

We were victims of changing circumstances while putting together this book. We collected together a lovely little set of Heather McCartney jokes, and the silly wench goes and instigates divorce proceedings, hence mucking them all up. See this as an historical record.

It must be hard being a Beatles wife, it can't be a coincidence that most of these jokes are directed at them.

…But then, Paul McCartney is the nation's new Queen Mum.

A journalist interviews Sir Paul McCartney about his knighthood:

'So, Sir Paul, do you think that you will ever go down on one knee again?'

Paul: 'Oi! Her name is Heather.'

But remember her this way…

Paul McCartney bought his wife a new artificial leg this Christmas but it wasn't her main present, it was just a stocking filler.

For her birthday Paul McCartney is buying his wife a plane, but she'll still use a razor on the other leg.

What's got three legs and lives on a farm in Scotland?

Mr and Mrs McCartney.

Before Heather there was Linda…

What do you call a dog with wings?

Linda McCartney.

What do vegetarian worms eat?

Linda McCartney.

Paul McCartney tells his kids some bad news and some good news:

'The bad news is your mother's dead, but the good news is that it's bacon for tea tonight.'

And finally…

What does it take to re-unite The Beatles?

Two bullets. *(This punchline used to be 'three' but old misery guts Harrison ruined the joke by going and dying on us.)*

What's yellow and lives off dead beetles?

Yoko Ono.

**What's black and sits
at the top of the stairs?**
*Stephen Hawking after
a house fire.*

Christopher Reeve

Oh the irony, Superman ends up in a wheelchair.
Now that he's dead, you may wish to note that Reeve jokes are
interchangeable with Steven Hawking jokes, or any poor git
who ends up in a wheelchair.

Why didn't Superman stop the World Trade Centre attacks?

Because he's a quadriplegic.

What's the opposite of Christopher Reeve?

Christopher Walken.

15

Celebrity paedophiles

Our lawyers wouldn't let us actually use the names of any celebrity paedophiles in this section… Spoilsports.
So, we've left a space for you to insert your own favourite celebrinonce. Have fun!

What did the woman say to _____ on the beach?

'Can you move please, you're in my son.'

What's blonde, had six legs and ran through _____'s dreams?

Hanson.

Did you hear about _____'s latest holiday destination?

He's going to Tampa with the kids.

_____'s house was raided recently by a police drug squad. They found incriminating evidence everywhere: Class A in the kitchen, Class B in the bathroom and Class 4C in his bed.

What do whiskey and _____ have in common?

They both come in small tots.

Why does _____ like sex with twenty eight year olds?

Because there are twenty of them.

What's the difference between _____ and acne?

Acne doesn't come on your face until you are 13.

_____'s wife has just given birth. _____ asks the doctor how long it will be before he can have sex.

The doctor says, 'For fuck's sake _____ at least wait until it can walk'.

Why did _____ phone Boyz II Men?
He thought they were a delivery service.

What does _____ have after dinner?
Under Eights.

What do you call a paedophile pirate?
Yarr Kelly.

What is the worst thing about being _____?
You have to go to bed before 7.00 p.m.

What have Gary Glitter and Kodak film got in common?
They both come in a small yellow box.

What's the difference between greyhound racing and _____?
The greyhounds wait for the hare.

How do you know when it is bedtime at the _____ residence?
When the big hand touches the little hand.

_____ is sitting in his living room surfing the Internet on his laptop. All of a sudden, the door of the apartment whips open and his girlfriend storms through. She screams, 'You fucking asshole!' and heads into the bedroom. Stunned, _____ flips off the computer and walks toward the bedroom, wondering, 'Now what have I done?'.
Inside the bedroom he finds the girl furiously packing a suitcase. He asks her what's up. She responds with a hiss, 'My therapist says that I should leave you and that you're a paedophile!'. _____ responds, 'Wow, that's a pretty big word for an 8-year-old'.

_____ has been appointed as new England manager.

His first decision has been to put Seaman in the Youth team.

_____ has been made the new Dr Who.

His assistants will be K 9 and Sue, 12.

Helen Keller

Helen Keller was a deaf and blind woman whose story was told to countless school kids via the tear jerker movie The Miracle Worker. *We're very sorry to inform you that lots of those kids sniggered and made bad jokes about her and then emailed them to us. Ah well.*

Did you know that Helen Keller had a treehouse?

Neither did she.

What did Helen Keller's parents do when she was bad?

Leave the plunger in the toilet.

Why does Helen Keller wear tight jeans?

So people can read her lips.

What did Helen Keller say when she fell off the cliff?

Nothing. She had her mittens on.

Why did Helen Keller masturbate with one hand?

So she could moan with the other.

What did Helen Keller call her kids?

Muuurrghhrrhurrg.

**Did you hear about the cheese grater
Stevie Wonder's wife got him for his birthday?**
Most violent book he's ever read.

Stevie Wonder

Did you know that Stevie was blind? Ah, yes. We know that this is a stunning revelation, but please bear with us, there is a reason that we are telling you this: people can use this fact to make jokes. Actually, many of these jokes can be be rewritten for the famous blind person de jour: Ray Charles, David Blunkett and… er… many others too.

Why is Stevie Wonder always smiling?
He doesn't know he's black.

How did Stevie Wonder burn his ear?
The phone rang and he answered the iron.

How did Stevie Wonder burn his other ear?
They called back.

You ever seen Stevie Wonder's wife?
Neither has he.

What's black and loud?

Stevie Wonder answering the iron.

Stevie Wonder is playing his first gig in Tokyo and the place is absolutely packed to the rafters. In a bid to break the ice with his new audience he asks if anyone would like him to play a request.

A little old Japanese man jumps out of his seat in the first row and shouts at the top of his voice, 'Play a Jazz chord! Play a jazz chord!'.

Amazed that this guy knows about the jazz influences in Stevie's varied career, the blind impresario starts to play an E minor scale and then goes into a difficult jazz melody for about 10 minutes. When he finishes the whole place goes wild.

The little old man jumps up again and shouts, 'No, no, play a Jazz chord, play a Jazz chord'.

A bit ticked off by this, Stevie, being the professional that he is, dives straight into a jazz improvisation with his band around the B flat minor chord and really tears the place apart. The crowd goes wild with this impromptu show of his technical expertise.

The little old man jumps up again, 'No, no. Play a Jazz chord, play a Jazz chord'.

Well and truly outraged that this little guy doesn't seem to appreciate his playing ability, Stevie says to him from the stage, 'OK smart ass. You get up here and do it!'.
The little old man climbs up onto the stage, takes hold of the mike and starts to sing…

'A jazz chord to say I ruv you…'

**What does Stevie Wonder's wife
do when they've had a fight?**

She rearranges the furniture.

**What goes… -Click-Click- 'Is that it?',
-Click-Click- 'Is that it?', -Click-Click- 'Is that it?'**

Stevie Wonder doing a Rubik's Cube.

What is the fastest thing on land?
Stevie Wonder's speedboat.

What is Stevie Wonder's favourite colour?
Corduroy.

Why can't Stevie Wonder read?
Because he's black.

**Stevie Wonder was in a horrendous
car accident the other week.**
His life flashed before his ears.

Endless love: Stevie Wonder and Ray Charles
playing tennis.

Dear, departed Diana

When Diana died there was a national outpouring of grief.
Were people crying for their lost princess or was it a cathartic
excuse to publicly wail about their own life problems?
Who can say. Meanwhile, some people just sat in the pub
making mocking jokes. Here is what they said.

Why was Diana drunk on the night of the crash?

She had a couple of pints of Carling in her.

Why did Princess Diana have a Mercedes?

She wouldn't be seen dead in a Skoda.

Why did Elton John sing at Princess Diana's funeral?

Because he was the only queen that gave a fuck.

**...and remember, there's always light at the end of the tunnel...
unless you're Princess Diana.**

What was the difference between Princess Di's driver and George Best?

George Best could take corners pissed.

What's the difference between Lady Di and Michael Hutchence?

Michael Hutchence was wearing his belt.

What do Princess Di and Ferrero Rocher have in common?

They both come out of France in a fancy box.

Why did Princess Diana cross the road?

She wasn't wearing her seat belt.

What do Princess Diana and Pink Floyd have in common?

Their last big hit was *The Wall.*

How did they know Princess Diana had dandruff?

They found her Head and Shoulders in the glove compartment.

Did you know that Princess Di was on the phone when she crashed?

She was also on the dashboard, the windscreen, the gearstick and the headrests.

Why is Princess Diana like the Queen Mum?

They both died pushing 102.

What would Princess Diana be doing now if she was still alive?

Scratching the fuck out of the lid of her coffin.

What's the Queen getting Fergie for Christmas?

A black Mercedes and a trip to Paris.

What's the difference between a Mercedes and Princess Diana?

A Mercedes will reach 40.

What did Princess Diana do when she heard the driver had been drinking?

She hit the roof.

What's the one word that could have saved Princess Diana's life?

'Taxi'

Prince Charles was out early the other day walking the dog.
When a passer-by said 'Morning',
Charles said 'No, just walking the dog'.

Apparently, at Diana's funeral the Queen Mother caught the bouquet.

What's the difference between Mother Teresa and Diana?

Around 5 days.

What were Diana's last words?

'Have you been dri-'

Make your Own

Oh Peter!
Peter Sutcliffe

1) Cut out Oh Peter™ character.
2) Cut out patented Oh Peter™ stand.
3) Fold stand and attach to characters reverse side.
4) Have fun attacking prostitutes in the Bradford / Leeds area.
5) Careful with your Hammer™ and £5 note - you might get caught!!

£5

In the news

How long does it take after a major disaster for the jokes to start coming? About 5 minutes we reckon…

What's red and white and swims on its side?
The Herald of Free Enterprise.

What have The Herald of Free Enterprise and a condom got in common?
They're both roll-on roll-off and they're both full of dead seamen.

Why is Concorde so expensive?
Because it delivers you straight to the hotel.

What's got three legs and goes 'woof'?
Piper Alpha.

No2 in the series
Make your Own

"She's at peace now"
Dr Shipman

I'm afraid she's just left us...

She's gone to a better place

Oh look. I appear to be in the Will. How lucky!.

PAGE 2
Grandma Peg

GRANDMA PEG

SHIPMAN

And in the immediate aftermath of the July London bombings:

How much did a One-Day Travelcard cost on 7th July?

An arm and a leg.

SWEARY SUDOKU

N		F			A			
	K	H		N	T	O		F
U			H					C
	T	A	K		N	H	O	U
F					O	K		
	U			C				
			T				A	
	A	U	N		H	C		T
	F	K		C				O

ENTER THE LETTERS

F U C K A T H O N

SO EACH LETTER APPEARS ONCE IN EACH SQUARE AND LINE UP AND ACROSS

Space shuttle

There have been two space shuttle disasters, Columbia in 2003 and Challenger in 1986. We are pretty sure that you could reuse these jokes if there is a third disaster in 2020.

What's the last recorded message on the space shuttle's black-box?

'Go on then, let the woman drive.'

What's NASA's official drink?

Seven Up on the rocks with a splash of Teacher's.

Why does NASA drink Sprite?

Because they can't get Seven-Up.

What does NASA stand for?

Need Another Seven Astronauts.

Hitler

There's just something about Adolf that's just funny. We think it's something to do with school history lessons where you had to take it all so seriously. Or maybe it's just the moustache. Whatever the truth, if you're a rubbish comedian, doing a quick Hitler impression always gets a laugh. And if you're reading this Freddie Starr, yes, we mean you.

Knock, knock

Who's there?

Guess

Guess who?

The Gestapo, Miss Frank. Now open ze door!

Knock, knock

Who's there?

Gestapo.

Gestapo who?

VE ASK ZE KVESTIONS! –SLAP–

What's the difference between Hitler and Paula Radcliffe?
At least Hitler tried to finish the race

How do you crucify a spastic?

On a swastika.

What's brown and hides in the attic?

The diarrhoea of Anne Frank.

Why did Hitler commit suicide?

He saw the gas bill.

My Grandad died in a concentration camp.

Really?

Yes, he fell out of his machine-gun tower.

I'll never forgive the Germans for the way they treated my grandpa during the war. Passed over for promotion, time and time again.

What do you do with a Jew with ADD?

Put him in a concentration camp.

Crossword clue: 5 down, Jewish baker (6)

Hitler walks into the meeting room and turns to his trusted staff, 'I want you to organise the execution of 10 000 Jews and two hedgehogs'. Everyone looks around the table and after a long silence Goering pipes up, 'Mein Führer, why do you want to kill two hedgehogs?'. Hitler smiles and turns to the rest of the table, 'You see, no one cares about the Jews'.

Three Jews win the lottery and scoop the £8m jackpot. They are getting ready to divvy up the cash and one says: 'Right, so that's £2 million to me, £2 million to each of you, and £2 million to the Germans'.

The other two reply, '£2 million to the fucking GERMANS? What the fuck for?'.

Says the first Jew, rolling up his sleeve: 'Well, they did give us the numbers'.

Sex
and
shit

Sex is a deeply uncomfortable experience for the British, so what do you do? Make jokes about it!

Why does Dr Pepper come in a bottle?

Because his wife is dead.

Did you hear about the man with five penises?

His pants fit like a glove.

Had my first blow job today.

... Five whiskeys and I still can't get rid of the taste.

What's blue and sticky?

Smurf cum.

What did Cinderella do when she got to the ball?

She choked.

What is the difference between a dog and a fox?

About five drinks.

Flowerpot men

Bill: 'Flobbly dobble obble oop?'

Ben: 'If you liked me that much, you'd swallow it.'

Bill and Ben are sitting in the bath:

Bill: 'Fwobble wobba wobble.'

Ben: 'If you do that again, I'm getting out.'

A paedophile and a small child are walking through the woods. It's very stormy, with lightning spearing the sky and crashing thunder. The child looks up at the paedo and says 'I'm scared'. The paedo says, 'You think you've got it bad?! I've got to walk back on my own!'.

Paedophiles

If you weren't fed up with molestation jokes already,
here's some more. Kids love 'em.

How do you know if a Catholic priest is a paedophile?

Ask him two questions:

'Are you Catholic?'

'Are you a priest?'

A father is in the bath with his 3-year-old son.

Child: 'Daddy, why is my willy different from yours?'

Father: 'Well son, for a start, yours isn't erect.'

I LIKE TO GO DOWN TO THE SCHOOLYARD AND WATCH ALL THE CHILDREN JUMP UP AND DOWN AND RUN AROUND, YELLING AND SCREAMING.....

OF COURSE, THEY DON'T KNOW I AM USING BLANKS.

A guy goes to the pharmacy. 'I need some condoms for my 11-year-old daughter', he says.

The pharmacist is shocked: 'Your daughter is sexually active at 11?'.

The guy says, 'Not really, she just lies there like her little brother'.

A man pulls up in his car beside a little boy.

He opens the door, holds out a brown paper bag of sweets and says, 'Hey kid, if I give you a sweetie, will you come in my car?'.

To which the kid replies, 'Gimme the bag and I'll come in your mouth'.

What do you do after having a baby?

Put its nappy back on.

Why do you feed a baby into a blender feet first?

So you can come on its face.

Which king had the most children?

Jonathan.

IS SHE LEGAL?

YOU BET YOUR ASS!

Why take chances? Be a DRIVING INSTRUCTOR

What's the worst thing about sex with a 5-year-old?

Getting the blood out of the clown costume afterwards.

What's the best thing about sex with a 5-year-old?

Getting to kick them to death in the woods afterwards.

What's green, hard and full of semen?

– (insert any young child who has recently been abducted here)

What's the best thing about fucking a 6-year-old girl?

You can flip her over and pretend she's a 6-year-old boy.

What's the best thing about fucking a 6-year-old boy?

You don't have to pretend!

What's the best thing about having sex with children?

Their tiny hands make your cock look big.

How do you make a 5-year-old cry twice?

Use her teddy bear to wipe the blood off your penis.

How do you know your sister's on her period?

Your dad's dick tastes funny.

What did the Jewish paedophile say to the little boy once he was in the car?

'Hey, go easy on the sweets, I'm not made of money!'

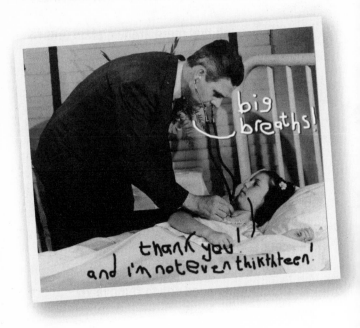

What's black and blue and afraid of sex?
The 8-year-old in my cellar.

What kind of file do you need to turn a 15-mm hole into a 40-mm hole?
A paedophile.

What do you call a toddler with a runny nose?
Full.

How can you tell that there are two elephants in your fridge?

You have to put the partly-eaten dismembered body parts of your infant daughter in the freezer instead.

Katie is 5 years old. Tomorrow will be her birthday.

'Dad, guess how old I'll be tomorrow?'

'Don't know,' he replies.

'I'll be six!'

She goes into the kitchen and sees her Grandad.

'Grandad, guess how old I'll be tomorrow?'

'To answer that I need you to remove your knickers.'

So she does that and he sniffs them. Then he fingers her, smells his finger and licks it.

'You will be six tomorrow,' he says.

'How do you know that?' she asks.

'I heard you talking to your dad.'

Royal
Turd Search

The Queen has deposited 25 shits in her majesty's toilet. Can you find her poophemisms?

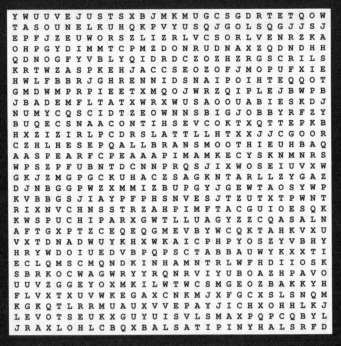

Ethiopians dinner	Turtle head	Caca
Bottom sausage	Dead otter	Botty slops
Turd	Number two	Rectum pate
Shit	Feces	Sphincter jizz
Poo	Anal stew	Bum eggs
Dump	Man pat	Downstairs unpleasantness
Crap	All bran smoothie	Sticky brick
Log	Big jobby	
Doodoos	Suspicious chocolate	

Scatological

Our jokes are shit. Literally.
…Did you see what we did there? Did you?

Why did the baker have smelly hands?

Because he kneaded a poo.

Little boy: 'Mummy, mummy, can I lick the bowl clean?'
Mother: 'No, just flush it like everyone else.'

What's the difference between a rectal thermometer and an oral thermometer?

The taste.

A teacher is reading a story to her class of infants, when she notices a wet patch all around a little girl.

Teacher: 'Oh! Katie, why didn't you put your hand up?'
Katie: 'I did Miss! But it trickled through my fingers.'

How did the constipated mathematician relieve himself?

He worked it out with a pencil.

Misogyny

Ooh look! We've used a posh word for sexism. Get us and our fantastic vocabulary.

BTW: Our favourite sexist lyric is Kool G's 'Chicks are on my dick like a human shish kebab'. Nice work if you can get it.

How do you get a fat girl into bed?
Piece of cake.

I like my women the way I like my coffee: ground up, in my freezer.

What's it called when a woman is paralysed from the waist down?
Marriage.

Why do women have legs?
Have you seen the mess snails make?

An undertaker says to a bereaved husband, 'When did you realise your wife was dead?' 'Well,' he replies, 'the sex was the same but the dishes just kept piling up…'

What's the difference between an onion and a dead hooker?

I cry when I cut up onions.

What has eight legs and makes women scream?

Gang rape.

What's black and eats cunt?

Cervical cancer.

What do you do when the dishwasher stops working?

Smack her across the face.

What's the difference between a washing machine and a 15-year-old girl?

The washing machine won't follow you around for two weeks after you drop a load in it.

What's the smartest thing to have come out of a woman's mouth?

Einstein's cock.

How many feminists does it take to change a light bulb?

Two: one to change the light bulb, the other to suck my cock.

Why do women wear make-up and perfume?

Because they're ugly and they smell.

What do you call a Serbian prostitute?

Slobberdownmycockyoubitch.

What's the best thing about kinky sex?

Wiping the blood off the hammer.

What's the best thing about sex with a dead hooker?

You don't have to pay her.

What's the difference between a woman and a computer?

You only have to punch the information into a computer once.

What's the first thing a beaten wife should do after coming back from hospital after the last 'incident'?

The dishes, if she knows what's good for her.

What do you call a lesbian with long fingernails?

Single.

What should you do if a bird craps on your car?

Never take her out again.

A man walks into a lift, which already has a very attractive woman in it.

As the lift is going up he asks, 'Excuse me miss, can I smell your fanny?'.

'Certainly not!' came her astonished reply.

'Ah! It must be your feet then.'

What do you call ten vaginas stacked up on top of each other?

A block of flaps.

3 vampires sitting
at a bar

the first two order
pints of blood

Noticing their friend
wasn't drinking
they asked him why?

Pulling out a Tampon
he says,
'Having Tea!'

prodigy69

Menstruation

Fact: men are scared of women's bits.
Fact: men make jokes about it to cover their fear.
Fact: women know this and find it pathetic.

What did one lesbian vampire say to the other?
'See you next month.'

What's the difference between a French woman and a basketball team?
The basketball team showers after four periods.

What's red and white and sits in a tree?
A sanitary owl.

Why do elephants have trunks?
Because sheep don't have string.

Why do women have periods?
Because they fucking well deserve them!

What has two legs and bleeds?
Half a dog.

Why do tampons have strings?
So you can floss after you eat.

What's the difference between a pitbull and a woman with PMS?
Lipgloss.

How did the Red Sea get its name?
Cleopatra used to bathe there periodically.

H 1 Hucknalls								
Li 3 Leaky insides	**Be 4** Burgund y eggs							
Na 11 Nether-meats anger	**Mg 12** Minge glue							
K 19 Kunt-ensheisse	**Ca 20** Compulsory anal	**Sc 21** Slot clot	**Ti 22** Twunty irritables	**V 23** Vaginals	**Cr 24** Camel retch	**Mn 25** Menstrual nutella	**Fe 26** Fanny excretia	**Co** Crim oth
Rb 37 Ruby blowhole	**Sr 38** Slippery runway	**Y 39** Yamjam	**Zr 40** Zebra rape	**Nb 41** Notch blood	**Mo 42** Minge OXO	**Tc 43** Twat curd	**Ru 44** Rusty under-pants	**Rh** Rag haem ph
Cs 55 Cunt shit	**Ba 56** Bloody axewound	**La 57** Ladies' angst	**Hf 72** Haem-ophiliac funburger	**Ta 73** Tush acne	**W 74** Washday	**Re 75** Red emulsion	**Os 76** Oyster slops	**Ir** It's
Fr 87 Fanny rot	**Ra 88** Ranc-orous abattoir	**Ac 89** Aborted child	**Rf 104** Ruddied froth	**Db 105** Dirt bubbles	**Sg 106** Sunday grots	**Bh 107** Beetroot herpes	**Hs 108** Hairy soup	**M** Mor titw

Ce 58 Chris Evans's	**Pr 59** Putrid runcibles	**Nd 60** Nubbin drops	**Pm 61** Party minge	**Sm 62** Sexy monthlies
Th 90 Twat haem-orrhage	**Pa 91** Penetrate anally	**U 92** Un-useable	**Np 93** Nob paint	**Pu 94** Painted under-carriage

Sir! I can't do games today - I am on the HUCKNALLS.

's

ABLE

DIA OF
SMS

					He 2
					Hufty's ectoplasm

B 5	C 6	N 7	O 8	F 9	Ne 10
Blob	Clots	Niagras	Ooze	Flow	Nash epilepsy

Al 13	Si 14	P 15	S 16	Cl 17	Ar 18
Angry lips	Slit Injury	Paint	Sputter	Cunt lipstick	Anchovy rasp-berries

28	Cu 29	Zn 30	Ga 31	Ge 32	As 33	Se 34	Br 35	Kr 36
ch k	Cunt umbridge	Zero nookie	Gash ache	Gyne-cological enema	Axe-wound sludge	Snatch enchilada	Bloody rag	Krusty ringpiece

46	Ag 47	Cd 48	In 49	Sn 50	Sb 51	Te 52	I 53	Xe 54
nty rt	Angry growler	Cunt discharge	Intermin-able nastiness	Stinky noggin	Sullied beaver	Titian emission	Ick	Xylo-phone explosion

78	Au 79	Hg 80	Tl 81	Pb 82	Bi 83	Po 84	At 85	Rn 86
g-cy st	Auburn undies	Haemo-globin goblins	Tainted labia	Piss blood	Bitter ichor	Parson's Ooze	Acrid tapenade	Rancid niff

10	Rg 111	UUb 112	Uut 113	Uuq 114	Uup 115	Uuh 116	Uus 117	Uuo 118
lical ry	Russet gusset	Utterly unctuous beaver	Unending uterus trauma	Useless umbilical quagmire	Ulrika's unusual piss	Un-available, use hooters	Unwante d uterine slush	Unfort-unate undersid e ooze

Gd 64	Tb 65	Dy 66	Ho 67	Er 68	Tm 69	Yb 70	Lu 71
Galloping drizzlies	Treacle biscuits	Damson yogurt	Horrific overflow	Eggy rouge	Torrential minge	You're bleeding!	Leaky uterus

Cm 96	Bk 97	Cf 98	Es 99	Fm 100	Md 101	No 102	Lr 103
Clit muck	Baby ketchup	Chuff frapp-achino	Edam squits	Foaming montyls	Muff damage	No oral	Labia rot

75

SCI-FI SWEARS

Match up these fictional expletives with the science fiction show.

Boned! **Frak!** **Frag!**

Frek! **Frinx!** **Zark!**

Babylon 5

Star Trek: Deep Space Nine

BATTLESTAR GALACTICA

FARSCAPE

THE HITCHHIKER'S GUIDE TO THE GALAXY

FUTURAMA

What your score says about you:
0: You are a woman
1: You're a normal bloke
2: You've 'battle re-enacted'
3: You've had a Klingon wedding
4: You are William Shatner
5: You can't score five, you've broken the quiz
6: You're 47 and live with your mum

Answers:
Boned! - Futurama
Frak! - Battlestar Galactica
Frag! - Babylon 5
Frek! - Farscape
Frinx! - Star Trek: Deep Space Nine
Zark! - The Hitchhiker's Guide to the Galaxy

Anti-men

Anyone who says they hate men just needs a good seeing to with a big hard cock.

Women of 35 think about having children. What do men of 35 think about?

Fucking children.

What did God say after creating man?

'I can do better.'

Two guys were strolling down the street when one guy exclaimed, 'How sad – a dead bird'.

The other man looked up and said, 'Where?'.

How do you scare a man?

Sneak up behind him and start throwing rice.

Why is it so hard for women to find men that are sensitive, caring and good-looking?

Because they already have boyfriends!

How do you get a man to do situps?

Glue the TV remote between his ankles.

Why do black widow spiders kill their mates after mating?

To stop the snoring before it starts.

How was Colonel Sanders a typical male?

All he cared about was legs, breasts and thighs.

What makes men chase women they have no intention of marrying?

The same urge that makes dogs chase cars they have no intention of driving.

What do men have in common with toilet bowls, anniversaries and clitorises?

They miss them all.

What do you have when you have two little balls in your hand?

A man's undivided attention.

How is a man like a snowstorm?

Because you don't know when he's coming, how many inches you'll get or how long it'll stay.

What do you call a man with half a brain?
Gifted.

Husband: 'Want a quickie?'
Wife: 'As opposed to what?'

Why do men find it difficult to make eye contact?
Breasts don't have eyes.

Why do men want to marry virgins?
They can't stand criticism.

I went to the County Fair. They had one of those 'Believe it or not?' shows.
They had a man born with a penis and a brain.

Why do men name their penises?
Because they want to be on a first-name basis with the person who makes all their decisions.

Did you hear the one about the man who won the gold medal at the Olympics?
He had it bronzed.

Why do men like masturbation?
It's sex with someone they love.

Loner Card

In the event of my Death, nobody is gonna give a shit, so why bother carrying this?

If you do find me, chances are it'll be in my bedsit, surrounded by copies of 'Mayfair' and 2 litre bottles of 'White Lightning'

PORN STASH DONOR CARD

I _____ having had no friends at all in my sad, pathetic, miserable and totally lonely existence on this planet, do hereby allow the following items to be harvested in the event of my death.

☐ All 245 copies of 'Big Jugs Monthly' (Used)

☐ My entire 'Star Trek TNG' DVD Collection

DONOR SIGNATURE _____

WITNESS (optional) _____

Husband: 'I don't know why you wear a bra, you've got nothing to put in it.'

Wife: 'You wear briefs don't you?'

What is gross stupidity?

144 men in one room.

Why did God create man?

Because a vibrator can't mow the lawn.

Why is an impotent man like a Christmas tree?

They both have balls for decoration.

Why don't women blink during foreplay?

They don't have time.

Why does it take 1 million sperm to fertilize one egg?

They won't stop to ask directions.

What do electric toy trains and breasts have in common?

They're intended for the children, but it's the men who end up playing with them.

What do men and sperm have in common?

They both have a one-in-a-million chance of becoming a human being.

Gay

There's a theory that homophobia comes from men who can't accept that they are subconsciously attracted to men. Who cares! Bummers are funny. Argh! Does that make us gay? Fantastic, then we can make gay jokes with impunity!

What's the first symptom of AIDS?

A sharp stabbing pain in the rectum.

How do you know if your best mate's gay?

He gets a hard-on when you fuck him up the arse.

How many homosexuals does it take to put in a light bulb?

Only one... but it takes an entire Emergency Room to get it out.

**How do you get a gay man to shag
your girlfriend?**

Shit in her cunt.

What did one homosexual say to the other in a bar?

'Pardon me, but can I push in your stool?'

How do you get four homosexuals on a bar-stool?

Turn it upside down.

What did one lesbian frog say to the other lesbian frog?

'They're right, we DO taste like chicken!'

What do you call a Lesbian with large fingers?

Well-hung.

What do you call a group of lesbians in a field of dildos?

Squatters.

Why are ghosts gay?

They put the willies up each other.

What do you call an Irish lesbian?
Gaelic.

What do you call an Indian lesbian?
Minjeeta.

What is the hardest thing about roller-blading?
Telling your parents you're gay.

COCK BUSTERS

1. What F describes a kangaroo's bifurcated meat flute?
2. What BW has a six and a half foot cock?
3. What M describes the medical condition possibly known as "Baddiel's Syndrome"?
4. What PS did John Wayne Bobbitt become after his wife cut off his old chap?
5. What L is cut to add two inches to the visible length of a nob?
6. What SF invented penis envy?
7. What N describes men who remove their own love truncheon?
8. What PEP is being sold in the 90% of spam that isn't about watches?
9. What C should you eat after having a wank to help prevent blindness?
10. What KT game does Moby like playing with fellow celebrities?
11. What M performs ritual circumcisions on Jewish babies?
12. Which DD was the large-cocked hero of the movie Boogie Nights?
13. What P describes someone with permanent erection?
14. Which GM waved his cock with gay abandon at the LAPD?
15. Which PA gave his name to a ring inserted into a foreskin to make sure a gentleman dresses on the left?
16. Which D is a famous, if rather under-endowed statue?
17. What SI is the average size of a dick?

Answers:
1. F: Forked
2. BW: Blue Whale
3. M: Micropenis
4. PS: Porn star
5. L: Ligament
6. SF: Sigmund Freud
7. N: Nullo. Or nutters
8. PEP: Penis Enlargement Pills.
9. C: Carrot
10. NT: Nob touching
11. M: Mohel
12. DD: Dirk Diggler
13. P: Priapic
14. GM: George Michael
15. PA: Prince Albert
16. D: David
17. SI: Six inches

What your score says about you:

0: I'll have an E please bob.

1 - 5: Scunthorpe Polytechnic studying biscuit technology.

6 - 10: You can probably still do the silly hand dance the audience did for the theme tune. Go on, have a go, you deserve it.

11 - 15: Smart enough to know that Bob Holness didn't play the saxophone solo on Baker Street.

16+ You are Ruth Lawrence.

C

PEP   KT

N   M

SF   DD

L   P

PS   GM

M   PR

BW   START   YOU ARE A WIN   D

F   SI

The Vicarage

 And GOD morning to you Mrs. Taylor! Ho ho!

Oh Vicar, you do make an old lady lau..

"sniff sniff"

 That smell.. Is that..

Urine?

 If I may consult the Good Book..

"Thou shalt not urinate"

But... But you've just crossed out 'steal' and wri-

Burn, Mrs. Taylor.

Waahh!

Religion and racism

As Depeche Mode once said, 'People are people so why should it be, you and I should get along so awfully?'

Kän yöu see vöt it ist yet?

Jewish

We never understood why Hitler gassed the Jews. Jews are useful... not like the French. He should have gassed the French.

How do you know if you're in a Jewish household?

There's a fork in the sugar bowl.

Why do Jews have big noses?

Air is free.

Why do Jews have double glazing?

So their kids can't hear the ice cream van.

What happens when a Jew with an erection walks into a wall?

He breaks his nose.

What's the definition of a queer Jew?

Someone who likes girls more than money.

What's black and white
and can't turn round in corridors?
A nun with a javelin through her head.

Christian

Seeing as we're having a go at the Jews and Muslims, it's only fair to take a pop at the God-squad. We're equal opportunity bigots you see.

Why is the Bible like a penis?

You get it forced down your throat by a priest.

Why can't Jesus eat M&Ms?

He has holes in his hands.

What's the difference between Jesus and a picture of Jesus?

It only takes one nail to hang a picture.

How do you get a nun pregnant?

Rape her.

What's black and white and tells the Pope to fuck off?

A nun who's won the lottery.

MR INTOLERANT

Muslim

While we were talking to our publishers about the possibility of making this book, the Jyllands-Posten Muhammad cartoons controversy broke. They said, 'please no Muslim jokes, we don't want to be fire-bombed'. So if this bit doesn't get snipped, let it be known that The Friday Project are a lovely and brave bunch of boys and girls who will be sorely missed.

What's the difference between Muslim extremists and Smarties?

Smarties don't blow up in the tube.

Two Muslim extremists walk into a bar.

Boom! Boom!

A man walks into a sex shop and tells the woman behind the counter he's looking for a blow-up doll. The woman asks, 'Would you like a Christian or a Muslim doll?'. Confused, the man says, 'What's the difference?'.

'Well,' replies the woman, 'the Muslim one blows itself up.'

Buddhism

Are Buddhists funny? Now and zen… Oh Christ! Who writes this drivel? Us? Sack us now!

Did you hear the one about the Zen Buddhist who called to order a pizza?

He said, 'Make me one with everything'.

The pizza delivery man hands the Buddhist the pizza, who pays with a £20 note. The delivery man starts to walk away, when the Buddhist stops him and asks for his change. The delivery man replies, 'Change comes from within'.

Why can't the Buddha vacuum under the sofa?

Because he has no attachments.

Ginger

Oh pity the poor ginger, your best role model is Mick Hucknall and both Catherine Tate and South Park are running regular period-head mocking japes. So kids, say it loud! You're ginger and proud!

A woman has just given birth in the hospital.
When she wakes up from a long sleep the doctor approaches her.
'I have some good news and some bad news…'
'What do you mean?!'
'I'm afraid your baby has ginger hair.'
'That's the bad news?! What's the good news?'
'He's dead.'

… Just watched that Harry Potter film, but it's pretty unrealistic. I mean… a ginger kid with two friends.

What do you call a ginger Goth?
Duracell.

White trash and chavs

Does anybody admit to being a chav? Only middle-class media types writing filler for the Guardian, 'Oh, I'm a chav, actually'. See how well that goes down in a boozer on the Old Kent Road.

What do you call a white guy dancing?
A seizure.

A chav girl goes to the doctor complaining of a strange green rash on her inner thighs.
The doctor takes one look and says, 'Tell your boyfriend his gold earrings are fake'.

What key can open any lock?
A pi-key.

What's green and gets a chav pissed?
A Giro.

What do you say to a chav when he's at work?
'Big Mac and fries please.'

What is the chav boy next door getting for Christmas?
Your bike.

What do you call a chav in a suit?
The accused.

What do you call a chav with an A-level?
A liar.

Two chavs race off the edge of a cliff. Who wins?
Society.

What do you call a chav in a white shell suit?
The bride.

Two chavs in a car without any music, who's driving?
The police.

What do you call a 30-year-old chavette?
Granny.

What do you call a chav at college?
The cleaner.

What do you call a chav on fire?
Blazin'.

You're in your car and you see a chav on a bike, why should you try not to hit him?
It might be your bike.

What do you call a knife in chav-ville?
Exhibit A

What do you call a chav in a tastefully decorated house?
A burglar.

What do chavs use as protection during sex?
A bus shelter.

Chinese

*The basic Chinese joke for beginners: Ls sound like Rs.
More advanced practitioners might like to use their fingers to
stretch their eyes diagonally. Yep, you are that low.*

Why do you get so many Chinese people in Harrow?

Because they get off the airplane, into the cab and say 'HARROW!'

What do you call a Chinese child molester?

Fuckum Yung.

What's the definition of a clunt?

Someone who runs away from a Chinese chip shop without paying.

The Welsh joke

Wales is a lovely place and we daren't say anything nasty about it as the official b3ta dad lives outside Cardiff and we don't want him knee-capped by the Taffia.

An Englishman, Welshman and West Indian are in hospital, waiting for their wives to give birth. There is quite a bit of pacing up and down when the nurse comes out and happily announces that they are all fathers of bouncing baby boys.

'There's just one problem,' she says. 'Because they were all born at the same time we got the tags mixed up and we don't know which baby belongs to whom. Would you, as their fathers, mind coming to identify them?'. The men agree and walk into the delivery room and look at the babies.

Immediately the Englishman stoops down and picks up the black baby. 'Yes, this is definitely my baby,' he says confidently. 'Um, excuse me,' says the West Indian, 'but I think it's fairly obvious that this is my son.' The Englishman pulls him aside and says, 'I see where you're coming from mate, but one of these babies is Welsh and I'm not prepared to take the risk'.

✉ SMS
15.03.06 19:16
Sorry i've not been
in touch. there was
a blackout on our
street & we weren't
allowed out til they
shot the cunt. <3
mum

Edit ✔ Options

Black

When we started putting this book together people said, 'You are not racists, surely you're not going to run black jokes?'. Well, if we're going to use spaz jokes, Jew jokes and ginger jokes then it would be unfair to leave the darkies out just because they're black. That, chum, would really be racist.

What is the difference between a black man and a bicycle?

A bicycle doesn't sing when you put chains on it.

Why don't black people dream?

The last one who had a dream got shot.

What's brown and runny?

Linford Christie.

What do you call a 3-foot-tall black person?
A Yardie.

What do you call a black man flying a plane?
A pilot, you racist.

Have you heard about Evel Knievel's latest stunt?
Riding through Ethiopia with a pork pie on his head.

Two black women with babies at a bus stop.
One says: 'Is yours teething yet?'
Other one says: 'Yes, he's managed to get two car stereos and a handbag.'

Irish

On our website we once ran a competition called 'If adverts told the truth'. Best entry? 'Guinness. It makes you fat and turns your shit black.'

What happened to the Irish terrorist who tried to blow up a bus?

He burnt his mouth on the exhaust pipe.

How do you get a one-armed Irishman out of a tree?

Wave.

Why wasn't Jesus born in Ireland?

Because they couldn't find three wise men or a virgin.

What did the Irishman call his pet zebra?
Spot.

Why did the Irishman wear two condoms?
To be sure, to be sure.

How do you sink an Irish submarine?
Knock on the hatch.

How do you get an Irishman on the roof?
Tell him drinks are on the house.

Two Irishmen are sitting on the ground.
One falls off.

How do you stop an Irish tank?
Kill the blokes pushing it.

'Well, it did get pretty boring up there'

Illness and mortality

As you get older you realise that there is nothing more important to your happiness than your health.
...Well, that and fags and drink.

OBSESSIVE
COMPULSIVE
DISORDER
SUPPORT GROUP

RING THE BELL

RING THE BELL

RING THE BELL

RING THE BELL

RING THE BELL

RING THE BELL

Disability

Have we offended everyone yet? Who have we missed out?
Send your emails to the Daily Mail and hopefully we'll get some
publicity for this tawdry collection of PC-baiting nonsense.
Actually, we know a Daily Mail employee and we asked him what
he thought they would make of our little book. 'Oh, they'll love it.
They love anything anti-PC. It's the liberal media who are more
likely to get into a huff about this stuff.' So there you go.

How did the quadriplegic fall off the cliff?

He was pushed.

Man goes to the ticket office at the railway station.

Man: 'Can I have a segond glass return do Dottinghab please?'

Ticket clerk: 'Sorry I don't understand.'

Man: 'Can I have a SEGOND GLASS REDURN TO DODDINGHAB PLEASE?'

Ticket clerk: 'Ahh, I see, have you tried Tunes sir?'

Man: 'Why, do they cure cerebral palsy?'

What's the smallest pub in the world?
The Thalidomide Arms.

They say whatever doesn't kill you makes you stronger.
Try telling that to someone with muscular dystrophy.

Did you hear about the thalidomide porn star?

He had an arm like a baby's cock.

What did the mongoloid say to his dog?

'Down, Syndrome!'

What's the best way to fuck a paraplegic?

Slash his tyres.

What sits at the end of your bed and takes the piss?

A kidney dialysis machine.

What goes MARK MARK?

A dog with a hair lip.

Three pregnant women sitting outside a doctor's surgery. They're all knitting in expectation of their new kids' imminent arrival. The first one takes out a tablet, pops it in her mouth and the others enquire as to its nature. 'It's a calcium supplement so my baby's bones grow nice and strong,' she replies and carries on knitting. The second woman also pops a pill and answers the same question with 'It's vitamin C to ward off colds and boost its immune system,' and also carries on knitting. The final woman takes a tablet but when she's asked what it is she replies, 'Thalidomide'. The other two are horrified and demand to know the reason for taking it. She replies 'I can't do sleeves.'

A spastic goes to an ice cream van. The man in the van asks him what flavour he'd like. 'Doesn't matter, I'm just going to drop the fucker anyway.'

How do you know when the vegetables are boiled?

The wheelchairs float to the top.

What's the hardest part of the vegetable to eat?

The wheelchair.

What do you call a wheelchair on top of a wheelchair?

A vegetable rack.

What's better than winning Gold at the Paralympics?

Having legs.

How many kids with ADHD does it take to screw in a light bulb?

Wanna go bike riding?

Two dyslexics walk into a bra.

What do you call an epileptic in a vegetable patch?

A seizure salad.

How do you get a leper out of the bath?

With a sieve.

What's a leper's favourite chocolate bar?

Flake.

What is hairy and has five fingers?

A thalidomide's armpit.

What do you give a thalidomide for Christmas?

A T-shirt and cuff-links.

Stevie Wonder was in the pub telling everyone how great skydiving is. I asked him how did he know when to brace for impact and he replied, 'That's the easy bit – the dog's lead goes slack'.

Blind

We once went to a posh restaurant where they served food in the pitch-black. The meal was shite but the experience was awesome. You should try it sometime.

Why can't Ray Charles drive?

Because he's blind. *(Well, dead actually.)*

:: .::: .. :: .::: .::::
David Blunkett's resignation.

What's brown and bumps into tables?

Jordan's son.

What's white and sticky?

A blind man's eyes.

How do you drive a blind girl crazy?

Make her read a stucco wall.

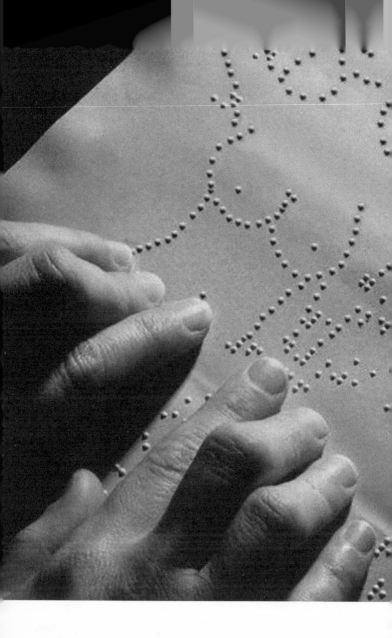

Porn for the blind

Cancer
vs. AIDS

A friend of ours thinks cancer is funnier than AIDS as science has virtually cured AIDS via combination drug therapy. 'It no longer has the sting it once has. Although AIDS was mainly funny because gays got it.' ...We need new friends.

What's black and has 17 tits?
The binbags behind the breast cancer ward.

What did the blind, deaf and dumb kid get for Christmas?
Cancer.

What can turn a fruit into a vegetable?
AIDS.

Doctor: 'It's bad news, you have cancer and Alzheimer's.'
Patient: 'Oh well, it could be worse – at least I don't have cancer.'

What are the three best things about Alzheimer's disease?
1. You make new friends every day.
2. You can laugh at all the old jokes.
3. You make new friends every day.

A woman visits her doctor complaining of a strange feeling in her lower stomach.
The doctor examines her and states, 'Well, I can tell you that you'll need to be buying lots of nappies in about 9 months' time'.
'Am I pregnant? That is wonderful news.'
'No, you have bowel cancer.'

Old people

*Here are some jokes to tell Grandad – assuming you've got one.
We don't want to offend anyone by bringing up the death of a
favourite relative or anything. We're sensitive souls you see.*

What's 100 yards long and smells of piss?
The Post Office queue on Thursday mornings.

What's blue and fucks old ladies?
Hypothermia.

What's blue and fucks old ladies?
The Conservatives.

What's got 100 balls and fucks old ladies?
Bingo.

What's blue and fucks grannies?

Me in my lucky blue coat.

Little Billy is sucking his Grandma's tit.
A touch of white stuff spurted into his mouth.
'Hey, Grandma,' said little Billy,
'Aren't you a little old to be producing milk?'
'Aw, Billy,' said his doting Grandmother,
'that isn't milk, it's cancer.'

How do you get a Granny to shout 'Cunt!'?
Get another one to shout 'Bingo'.

What's pink and smells of ginger?
Fred Astaire's fingers.

How do you make a Granny's toes curl?
Fuck her with her tights on.

What's pink and wrinkly and hangs out your grandad's underpants?
Your Grandma.

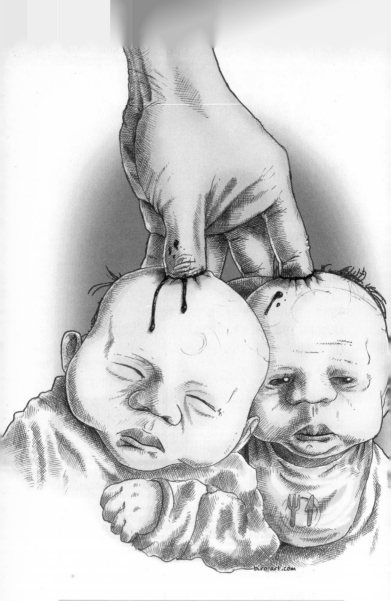

Why do newborns have holes in their skulls?
So you can carry them in fives, like beer cans.

Dead babies

We have a theory on dead baby jokes. They're for young kids who know that their mums wouldn't approve. However, if you become a parent yourself, then they stop being funny.

What's black and does your child's hair for you?

Leukaemia.

What's bright red-pink, 18 inches long, and makes women scream?

A parrot eating a baby.

What is red and bubbly and goes round and round banging on windows?

A baby in a microwave.

If there are 206 Bones in the Adult body

then how many are there in a Childs?

it all depends How HARD you Kick it down the stairs

What's pink and silver and runs around screaming?

A baby with a fork in each eye.

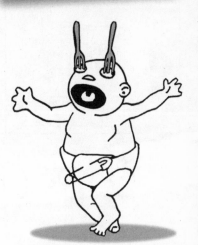

How do you make a baby drink?

Put it in a blender.

What's worse than a truck full of dead babies?

A truck full of dead babies with one live baby in the middle eating its way out.

What's red, slimy and crawls up a woman's leg?

A homesick abortion.

What sits quietly in the corner, getting smaller and smaller?

A baby with a cheese-grater.

What's red and pink and sits in the corner with its smile getting bigger and bigger?

A baby eating razor-blades.

What's purple, covered in pus and squeals?

A peeled baby in a bag of salt.

How do you make a dead baby float?

Add Coca-Cola and two scoops of ice cream.

What's blue, purple, pink, and sits in the corner?

A baby with an elastic band around its neck.

What is 12 inches long, pink and stiff, and makes women scream all night long?

Cot death.

What's black and blue and smokes in the corner?

A baby chewing on an extension cord.

What's white, round and fucks small children?

Aspirin.

How do you swat 200 flies in one go?

Hit an Ethiopian in the face with a frying pan.

What's blue and orange and lies at the bottom of a swimming pool?

A baby with burst arm bands.

Hear about the back-street abortionist whose business folded?

His ferret died.

What's the difference between a train carriage and a miscarriage?

You can't eat a train carriage.

What's the difference between a Ferrari and a pile of dead babies?

I don't have a Ferrari in my garage.

What's the difference between a dead baby and an apple?

I don't come all over an apple before eating it.

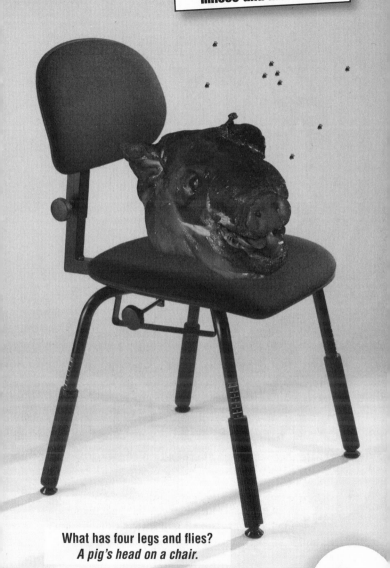

What has four legs and flies?
A pig's head on a chair.

SICKIPEDIA
Building the world's best collection of sick jokes, together

If you've got a sick joke that you think should have
been in this book, submit it to www.sickipedia.org
and if we ever make a sequel maybe you'll be in it.

Jokes with no home

Not all jokes have somewhere to live. Maybe you'll take these under your tender wing?

Anti-jokes

Jokes work by confounding your expectations. Some work by expecting you to know the punchline and going somewhere different. Like these little beauties.

What's grey and comes in pints?

My spunk.

What's yellow and tastes of piss?

Piss.

What's brown and sticky?

A stick.

Why does Noddy have a bell on his hat?

Because he's a cunt.

What did the deaf, dumb and blind kid get for Christmas?

A pinball machine.

SHEIK JOKES

How do you get a clown off a swing?
Hit him with an axe.

What do you get if you cross Billie Piper with a turkey?
Something horrible.

Knock knock!
Who's there?
Cancer!

Why did the girl fall off the swing?

Because she had no arms.

Police and hippies

*Gawd – this is nostalgia city. Remember the 1990s
and crusties? If these people still exist, these are the jokes
they're still telling.*

**What animal has a cunt in the middle
of its back?**

A police horse.

**What do you call a woman police officer who
shaves?**

Constable

What's orange and looks good on a hippie?

Fire.

One-liners

We've concentrated on jokes that are two liners. Here's others that didn't quite fit but we fancied sticking in anyway.

'Yes, Mrs. Lincoln, but did you enjoy the play?'

'I want to die in my sleep like my Grandad. Not kicking and screaming like his passengers.'

'Did you hear about the gynaecologist who decorated his house through the letter box?'

'It costs 10p to send this message. That's enough money for an African child to buy food and water to live on for a WHOLE DAY. Send this message to seven people and starve the cunt for a week.'

'A paraplegic walks into a bar. Only joking...'

'In today's news, police in Alabama found the body of black man hanging from a tree. His arms and legs had been cut off, he'd been set on fire and shot seven times. The Sheriff said it was the worst suicide he'd ever seen.'

149

TABBY

BORN AUG 1998

DIED DEC 2000
     FEB 2001
     JUN 2001
     NOV 2001
     SEP 2002
     MAY 2003
     OCT 2004
     FEB 2005
     APR 2006

Cruelty to animals

One of the first jokes we remember as a child was about the butcher shop with the sign, 'Watership Down. You've read the book, you've seen the film and now eat the pie'. All seems rather nostalgic now that rabbit meat has mostly dropped off the menu. On a similar note isn't Chas and Dave's line 'You've got more rabbit than Sainsbury's' a strange anachronism now?

A baby seal walks into a club…
Boom. Boom.

How do you stop a dog shagging your leg?
Suck its cock.

What's black and white and red all over?
Panda rape.

What's the difference between a cow and a hamster?

The cow survived branding.

What's got 100 balls and fucks rabbits?

A shotgun.

Two guys are walking down the street and see a dog on the lawn licking his balls.

So one guy says to the other, 'Man, I sure wish I could do that'.

The other guy says, 'Don't you think you ought to pet him first?'.

What do you call a deer with no eyes?

Bambi's mum.

No, Mr. Slug, I expect you to DIE!

What do you do if a kitten spits at you?

Turn the grill down.

What's yellow and smells of bananas?

Monkey sick.

What's got four legs and goes 'Miaow'?

A frozen dog on a bench saw.

How do you make a cat go 'Woooof!'?
Cover it in petrol and strike a match.

What's grey and comes in pints?

An elephant.

What is green and smells of pork?

Kermit's fingers.

What do you do if you come across a tiger in the jungle?

Wipe it off and apologise.

How do you make a dog go meeeoooowwww?

Tie it to a motorbike.

What do you do if an elephant comes through the window?

Swim!

Hello is that the pet shop?

I want to buy a kyttum please

Hello little girl. Yes we have a cute little ginger and a little fluffy tabby with cute pink eyes.....

Well actually, I don't think my python will give a fuck

What do elephants use as tampons?

Sheep.

What's green and red and goes round and round and round?

Kermit the Frog in a blender.

Google Mail – Compose Mail

`http://mail.google.com/mail/`

n eBay Yahoo! News (279) ▼ b3ta ▼ ⊗ Google Mail - Compose ...

es ⊗ Steal this book - Sick Jo... ⊗ Google Mail - Compose ...

Show search op
Create a filter

(Search Mail) (Search the Web)

e™
BETA

Discard | Draft autosaved at 5:22 pm

Send | Save Now |

To: stealthisbook@sickjokebook.com STEAL THIS

Add Cc | Add Bcc

Subject: fw: fw: fw: OMG LOL ROFL www.sickjokebook.com

The full text and images from this book are available at
www.sickjokebook.com

Yes that's right. All of it. Including this bit here.

If you like this book then tell your friends by forwarding the link.

Rob Manuel
www.sickjokebook.com

Send | Save Now | Discard | Draft autosaved at 5:22 pm

Poetry corner

We asked people to send us jokes, we didn't expect bloody poetry. However, we liked a few of them so here goes...

Jack and Jill went up the hill
So Jack could lick Jill's fanny
All he got was a mouthful of cum
'Cos Jill's a fucking tranny

Not quite a joke...

There was an old woman
Who lived in a shoe
She had so many children
Her cunt fell out

There once was a man from Nantucket
Whose dick was so long he could suck it
He said with a grin
As he wiped off his chin
'If my ear was a cunt, I would fuck it'

There was a young chap called Dave
Who kept a dead whore in a cave
He said, 'I admit
She does smell a bit
But look at the money I save'

I love my dog and he loves me
And that's the way love is supposed to be
But when it comes to having sex
'Woof Woof Woof!' barks my dog Rex

Mime jokes

Aha! This bit of the book is a little different. These are jokes for you to learn and play out to your friends in the pub with actions. They are our favourites you know.

How many shredded wheat does Superman eat for breakfast?

(Pause, stare at them, and blink twice.)

You're sitting in a pub. Ask your mates what a woman says after her first blow job. Take a sip of your pint as they ponder the answer, and retain the beer in your mouth. Pause for a few seconds. Then say 'I wuv you!' allowing beer to spurt everywhere.

Why was Jesus so popular with the ladies? Because he was hung like THIS.

(Adopt crucifix position, palms forward as if indicating penis size.)

How does Jesus masturbate?

(Silently hold hand out flat over crotch,
palm facing inward, and move hand in
and out in a waving gesture.)

How does Jesus masturbate?

(Assuming that your audience already knows
the joke, then here's an alternative ending,
Stretch arms out, as if on a cross and
make downward grabbing motions with
your mouth as if you're attempting to suck
yourself off. Extra points for miming frustration.)

What does the cum of a 12-year-old boy smell like?

(Exhale.)

What's this?

(Stick some paper money under your chin and dribble.)

Stephen Hawking at a titty bar.

What's this?

(Sit at an awkward angle and dribble.)

Stephen Hawking on being told his wife has died.

What's this?

**(Place your hands over your ears
and tap the ground with your foot.)**

An Irish mine detector.

I came this close to a blow-job last night

**(Hold thumb and forefinger a
centimetre apart.)**

(Bend over as far as you can and
try to reach crotch with your mouth.)

What's this?

**(Assume crucifix/cross position
with feet and legs firmly together,
and then swing arms and torso
in a bendy circular fashion.)**

Jesus on a rubber cross.

What's this?

**(Assume crucifix/cross position
with feet and legs firmly together,
neck slack in recently-deceased fashion.)**

A truly shit way to spend Easter.

What does a gay man say after sex?

(Let some frothy spit dribble out your mouth.)

What's this?

**(Rub your chin against each
shoulder whilst grinding your teeth.)**

Superman putting on his cape.

What's this?

**(Make wheelchair motion
with your hands, but occasionally
flick your head back.)**

The Paralympic Hurdles.

Can't be bothered to add you sick jokes to www.sickipedia.org? Write them here with a biro.

PANIC PAGE!

Take a breath. Think of the kittens. Think of the kittens. Take a breath. Think of the kittens. Take a breath. Think of the kittens. Take a breath. Think of the kittens. Take a breath. Think of the kittens.

How do you kill a circus?

Go for the juggler.

Why do elephants have big ears?

Because Noddy wouldn't pay the ransom.

What's a shitzu?

A zoo with no animals.

Why does Edward Woodward have so many D's in his name?

Because otherwise he'd be Ewar Woowar.

Where does Kylie buy her kebabs from?

Jason's doner-van.

Two cows in a field. One says, 'I'm not scared of mad cow disease'. The other says, 'Oh really, why not?'. The first replies, 'Because I'm a helicopter'.

Thanks to

None of this would be possible without Lucy,
David Stevenson, Rob Tinsley, Mike Trinder,
Fraser Lewry, Joel Veitch, Denise Wilton,
Steven D Wright, Jonathan Blyth, Robert Popper,
Cal Henderson, Tomsk and all at B4ta,
and Paul and Clare from The Friday Project

Jokes supplied by

earwaxuk, AdrianJ, alexr, Amazing Mr Strange,
animalsinclothes, asme, assistant commissioner
terra blanche, Avast, Axis: Bold as love, Bad Horsey,
badbadger, bakelit72, baldmonkey, barronshark,
Bearos, Beastie, beergut, bennyhillslovechild,
Bertie Dastard, bigbadtone, bilbobarneybobs,
Bill Stickers, blindspot, Bob Hopelessness,
BorderlineSchizo, boyx, busterbeckett, Butters,
Caligula, camel-related incident, Cap'n Tallbeard,
captain emo, Cashy, caspar_ghodd, CdrVimes,
Celebral, chalky_bumface, Charlie Baked Potato,

Charlie big bananas, Cheesemonger,
Cherry Dude, Chuckman, Citadel, ClockworkDespot,
cosmicmuffdivers, craddster, crayongirl, daddyk,
dani_B, Daveh, DeadCats, Dinsdale v Spiny Norman,
Dixon_Bawls, Dizzy Bob loves nuts, djgalaxe,
DoctorDeath, Dogmatix, Dooley, Durch Den Monsun,
DustyD, elgonzorelli, Elsie Charsnal, Eumphazard,
fatcatpat, ferret charmer, Fire and Forget, Fishgoth,
Flapjack, fox_handybread, fried gold, frogdoctor,
Gadzooks, Gaz, gedo69, geegee, gehenna, gentleben,
Ghost rider on a unicycle is on a unicycle, Gibber,
gizmo, Gizmo.MP3, grey kid, gronkpan, gstewart3000,
HairyBaldy, Haku, hot wee wee jefferson,
Humpty Dumpty was Pushed, I'm new!
chocapocalyptic, Insane Maniac, Jam Master Geordie,
jeccy, JKF, JLB8, Joel Roddy, johnny chode,
JohnPaulCassanova, jo-jo the majic clown,
jonnybignose, JonnyMX, Kage, kalimah,
Kaziko,KernKraft, king cnut- works for fcuk, kinks,
kiss_my_bunni, Kong, Kuroi Kyo, La Chockita,
Lamby, Lanc, Last Night A DJ Battered My Christ,
lat297, Laughing Boy, lightie, Limpy713, Llamanator,
lo, localknowledge, lohr, Lord Monkey of Yorkshire,
lordironlung, Loz, Lozhead, maiden, meatybrain,

Mehitabel_ltrang, mikek01, mindlouse, Mischeivious_Delinquent_Squirrel, misteroz1979, Mong-the-Merciful, monkdewallydehonk, monkeon, monkeymoo, Monskervator the Monsk, moorph69, Mr Slippyfist, Mr_Jums, mrbongo, muggins, Munsta, Mystery Woo Yay Boy, newcustomerserviceteam, newg, not_real had his name thieved, NotSaying, now restart, nufc, onewetleg, P45, pacificprincess1, pdjpdj, Phagenius, pointyearedpixie, poopascoopa, popey, pstafallen, Punkrockbilly, R. Jimlad, rabid peanut, racetraitor, rachboc, Rata-tat-atouille, ravabelli, REBELTRADING, Reid is the hotstepper, Rev. Otana, Rob Manuel, Roland E O'Dorant, ruud316, sarah sarah sarah, schnuff, Scoopzilla, scrumpydrinker, seanfish, setimret, Sheeps, shin0r, Sir T. Skellington, Skulk, slink, smashisimo, social hand grenade, Songi, Sorry, Soup and Toast, spacebaboon, Speccy, Spiteme, SpookTheHamster, Starzy, Stepping Hen the Delirious, Stinkfinger, Strawberry Dragon, Styxx, sugarplum, supermoore, swaza, syrtismajor, techierob, Thalidamide_Squirrel, that aint a monkey thats my wife, The Beast, The Duke of Prunes, The Great Architect, the Greebo Warrior, the magnificent mister birch, The Pink Strat Copy,

The spankster, the.gregster, The_Reaper, thefatsnowman, TheGords, thegripesofwrath, throatwobblermangrove, Todd Monotony, tomshave, tufty the chav slayer, Ultra, Ultra - Sitting drinking Cris' with my bitch Anne Frank!, urbane legend, V3lvetPresley, wcbal, We are the lemon, wez, Wibbly Pig, wingpig., witty_ditty, Wong Fei-Hung, Woodgie, Workboresme, Yarblesnake and zaitsevrogue9.

Period Table additional suggestions by

baldmonkey, Enigmatic, Art101, Godzuk, Neon Blue, Dr. Shambolic, Dr Jamuel Masterson of Geordie, Mr. Tea, Johnny Catfish, Flapjack - grey kid, printmeister, meagle, e p f, Felchman, Canazza, spong, Lightguy, friendlyfire, Fudgebags, bapsworld, first inch is the worst! CaL_FiN, Kersal Missive, Weetobix, ed.ge, Lanky, 5lab, doctorwhen, Legless I, WhoElse, spoonmuppet, Laughing Boy, dbond, Absynth&Cheese, EasyCheese, Oil of Ollie, calibrax, VampireMonkeyOnSpeed, printmeister, setimret, Rushy, Moel Siabod, knee deep in the hoopla, Fraser, writerblock, Mentallybizarre, smigga, Fizzle, Onion

Terror. DavyBoyInGravyJoy, Digeridude, darth munki, Wasp Box, Flowerpot, Jimtastic, MrFlump, Slinkachuu, porky, Sickpuppy, Bad Horsey, The Great Architect, Derek Monte, Dirtyleeds

Poems by

caspar_ghodd, CdrVimes, JonnyMX, Rob Manuel and Todd Monotony.

Illustration list

36/37 – Shipman by James Sandham – www.sandham.co.uk

38 – Sutcliffe's hammer by mushybees: www.mushybees.com

39 – 911 by carowallis: b3ta.com/users/profile.php?id=23627

40 – Sweary Sudoko by Boyx: www.boyx.co.uk

42 – Meinspace by FoldsFive: www.barbelith.co.uk

44 – Radcliffe by daddypigsaw: www.pigsaw.co.uk

45 – Gas by The Neville: www.nevillesgarden.co.uk

46 – Jewish baker by Thor_sonofodin: www.lulu.com/content/136766

48 – Englishman by Eddache: www.bolloxcomics.co.uk

52 – Thunder by Frunt: www.frunt.org

54 – Blanks by neilhillen: b3ta.com/users/profile.php?id=31822

56 – Legal by collapsibletank: b3ta.com/users/profile.php?id=29101

57 – Lucky day by Grey Kid: www.dearme.co.uk

58 – Big breaths by new_matt: www.5318008.co.uk

60 – Turd Search by Rob Manuel: www.b3ta.com

62 – Black eyes by Duphrates: www.duphrates.co.uk

64 – Sister by I was penalized for that: b3ta.com/users/profile.php?id=18273

98 – Hillbilly by prodigy69: prodigy69.myby.co.uk/prodigy69

104 – Black txt by thebasstard: b3ta.com/board/profile.php?id=28748

107 – KKK by Sunshine Elephant: www.monkeybackpack.co.uk

110 – Jesus happy fun time by Mugatu

112 – OCD by Darryn.R: www.themoononline.com

114 – Arms by DeKay: b3ta.com/users/profile.php?id=15793

115 – Adventures of… by Butters: madandugly.drunkrhino.com

116 – Mark mark by Frunt: www.frunt.org

118 – Wheelchair by Is it just me?: b3ta.com/users/profile.php?id=18587

119 – Eczema by Dixon_Bawls: b3ta.com/users/profile.php?id=24132

120 – Slack by Ash: www.madhousebeyond.com

122/123 – Porn by ashurek: www.tungsten-army.com/gallery.htm

124 – Bin bags by frogdoctor: b3ta.com/users/profile.php?id=17327

126 – Conga by Butters: madandugly.drunkrhino.com

129 – Blue coat by strawberrydragon: www.strawberrydragon.com

And special thanks to

Butters of http://madandugly.drunkrhino.com/ for
drawing the lovely flickbook thingie.